# More Praise for Ann Fisher-Wirth and *Blue Window*

"Tender and erotic, radiant and lyrical, these poems anoint life and death, and their beautifully fragile stories in between, with something like an Original Shine. "The light in me/greets the light in you." And it's true, the light in Ann Fisher-Wirth's work rushes forward to illuminate, animate, and redeem all that it touches. After this book, darkness becomes more bearable."
—Barbara Ras, *Bite Every Sorrow*

"Such power. Ann Fisher-Wirth has become the blue light. Always her poems bring me to tears, filled as they are with an awful beauty; they are elegiac, haunting, and like the soul, full of light and air. These poems are wild foxes that leave you staring at the invisible space in the green woods through which they disappeared."
—Janisse Ray, *Ecology of a Cracker Childhood*

"Ann Fisher-Wirth's debut collection of poems witnesses and sings the body electric with memory. In the poems set in Mississippi where Fisher-Wirth lives, her Whitmanic vision allows her to embrace the beauty of the woods and local people as well as to be a witness to its painful history, and thus to offer her poems as a healing. *Blue Window* is a beautiful blessing of a book."
—Sharon Dolin, *Heart Work*

# Blue Window

Poems

## Ann Fisher-Wirth

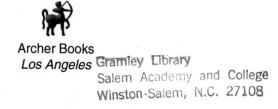

Archer Books
*Los Angeles*

Published in 2003 in the United States by
Archer Books
P. O. Box 1254
Santa Maria, CA 93456
www.archer-books.com - info@archer-books.com

Distributed in the United States by
Midpoint Trade Books, New York, NY
www.midpointtrade.com

First Edition

Printed in the United States

Cover image: Martin Dain, courtesy of the University of Mississippi

Cover design: JTC Imagineering

Library of Congress Cataloging-in-Publication Data

Fisher-Wirth, Ann W.
  Blue window : poems / by Ann Fisher-Wirth.
    p. cm.
  ISBN 1-931122-15-6 (pbk.)
  1. Girls--Poetry. 2. Women--Poetry. I. Title.

PS3606.I79B58 2003
811'.6--dc21

2002154562

For my family
—past and present—

# Contents

IV

V

# Acknowledgments

Many people and several institutions have helped to make this book a reality. An Artist Fellowship from the Mississippi Council for the Humanities, a tuition scholarship from the Squaw Valley Community of Writers Poetry Workshop, a residency at The Mesa Refuge, and summer grants from the University of Mississippi all gave me not only time to write but also a sense of community and encouragement in my writing. To them all I am very grateful.

I live among poets and readers of poetry, and from them I have received tough, wonderful feedback. For every help they have given me, my deep thanks to Aleda Shirley, my sister Jennifer MacKenzie, Mairéad Byrne, Salita Bryant, Beth Ann Fennelly, Blair Hobbs, and Athena Kildegaard, and most of all my husband Peter and my daughter Jessica, whose knowledge of poetry is vast and whose standards for poetry are exacting.

"It is a true error to marry poets / or to be by them," John Berryman writes in *The Dream Songs*. But I am a supremely lucky woman, whose family does not agree with him. This book, like my heart, is for them: for my mother, Irma Mitchell; my husband, Peter Wirth; and our five children, Pascale Fisher, Jessica Fisher, Lucas Fisher, Rebecca Wirth, and Caleb Fisher-Wirth.

I

# Blue Window

In that shadowy time before sorrow—
that twilight, October in Berkeley, the early 60's,

when I walked home along Euclid from Mrs. Runkle's
where I'd played Schumann's *"Traumerei"*

so beautifully, for once, I'd made her cry—
Before the missile crisis, when I sat on the bed in fear and exaltation

and thought of Anne Frank—while on the TV downstairs,
Soviet ships inched closer to Cuba—and wondered,

when they come to get me, when I hide beneath my desk,
my head in my hands, and the walls shake,

will I have told the world
how I love this life I am forced to lose?

Before Christian, my neighbor, drank developing fluid
and his death at Alta Bates took 48 hours, the poison dissolving his stomach,

and his father the beautiful philanderer told my mother,
"The divorce caused it," just failing to add, wringing

his elegant crooked fingers, "He did it for grief of me"—
before Ronnie, my neighbor, took acid and flew out a window,

and Jackie, my neighbor, drove 90 miles an hour into a stone wall
at prep school in Massachusetts, and Kwaasi, my neighbor,

talked to God and carved his arms and died at Napa,
the boys who lived around me lost, all dead by nineteen—

and before I had ever bled yet, ever got high, or
loved a boy, or played at kisses through Kleenex with Mary Lou—

In that time before my father lay in bed
all one year's end, the vast flower of his death blossoming,

and wrote, in a tiny crabbed hand, in the datebook I found years later,
"Had to increase the dosage today. Ann and Jink allowance"—

in that Christian Science household no one spoke, silence thickened upon us,
to this day no one has ever said to me, "It was brain cancer,"

but last winter my husband got drunk in his rare blind fury,
ran weeping into the room and pounded the bed over and over,

shouting, "Don't you understand yet?
In the war they treated men for lice with lindane,

poured it over their heads,
they did it to your father, and now the fuckers tell us

lindane eats your brain." —In that time, that twilight,
when I walked slowly home along Euclid,

how I wanted to belong to the family I saw
through the blue, wisteria-covered window, to be their girl,

enter their garlicky dinnertime kitchen,
later, to sit on a high attic bed, legs crossed tailor-fashion,

and pick dreamily at white chenille—
I wondered, why not be anyone, go anywhere?

when light dies around the oakleaves
and white, ragged moths come out to beat against the streetlight,

why not knock at the door and say "I am yours. I am here"?

# The Ways He Called Me

Then I was thirteen.
In my bedroom playing jacks
I nearly heard him call me.
Hand in the air, I waited.
I heard the oven door close,
mother murmuring in the kitchen.
Again the air moved
or did not move.
Later he came. I lay in bed
tracing the delicate hoop of my sex
over and over. He told me
that he loved me. Me, Ann. Spindrift,
will-o'-the-wisp, coffin of flesh.
He told me he would hold me
while I burned. He wanted me
to suffer and grow holy.

Or if he wanted me so much,
the brigand who came swaggering
and riding,
he could tip me in a ditch
beside the high road—its wet, thick grasses
steeped in sunlight
and sprinkled with forget-me-nots—
and he could rip the laces of my dress
and write his name with knives
in my soft, spilled breasts.

I would lie in a darkening room
while men came to me like water
till their bodies
taught me beauty—
artesian pulse
in the hollow of the throat,
secret life of cheekbones
and angelwings,
and the fine, soft fur
stirring alive beneath my fingers,
I cannot tell you how quietly—

# The Soft Black Cotton

Such eros in her demure. The soft black cotton
with furling crimson roses
shifted and pulled as she lifted her arms,

feeding towels, sheets, pillow cases, to the mangle's
steaming roller. I watched, transfixed,
the dovelike fall of her breast, then turned to my own

small ironing board and pressed her fifteen hankies.
Lace and embroidered violets, the curlicued
swooping $\mathcal{J}$ for her name. . . . We played Let's Describe

or Movie Stars. "Does your dream house have a ballroom?
Is your ballgown foam, with diamonds?
Who played the girl in 'National Velvet'?"

My world in her calm hands, the hours in the workroom
steadily rising, the warm forgetful round of her body.
Later, when I lay down calm with boys

and their frantic hearts beat into me, or when I
shut my eyes, my hair warm against their bellies,
and swallowed their bitter seed—and then when

she found out, drove me to the hills, parked on a cliff,
said, "If I had a gun I'd shoot us both"—
didn't she know I was being her daughter?

# Between Merced and Morning

In yourself, you're nothing—
a man in a three-piece suit
who buys me a drink
in a lounge car. But your initials

are my father's; the thin flaked gold
stamped into your leather briefcase
spells me his name.
Therefore I will take you,

therefore I will lie down with you,
here, this night, on this train. Take you
because when he died . . . ah,
man I hardly knew, he went everywhere,

he is smoke and fog and starlight.
Give me your hand, lay it
where my breath catches, where my heart
thuds in the blue wool dress

my mother bought me. Put down your glass,
come to my room, we'll lie close, spoons
on the fold-out berth, as dark fields,
darker strobes, *shoosh   shoosh* as we pass.

All night the train will fall through California.
And when you sneak away at dawn,
I will kneel on my bed as the miles pulse by,
gaze at my body in the shimmering mirror.

# To Answer

*For a college boyfriend, Dave*

After twenty-eight years I receive
an antique, sepia, scallop-edged card
showing King Arthur's Castle, Tintagel.
You do not sign, you have forgotten
how to spell my name.
You say she calls to you now.
The blue space of your words
spreads like circles when stones are dropped,
and the cove and looming cliffs, the headland
with its fortress
summon me like sleep. I return to the picture
again and again, as if to climb its path,
to find its hidden ocean.

      Why does she come to you now,
      the child we witched out of the darkness?
      Why does she trouble your sleep,
      her small perfect howl like a seabird's,
      crying on the wind, borne across
      the salt spray?

When you climbed up to my dormitory window,
I lay naked in the shadows.
What did we know of grief in the soft coal of that night?
Flagrant, shining, we barely made a sound
until the rainbirds came alive, toward dawn,
flinging their spray in widening arcs beneath the trees.

      But in that later room
      I clawed your back to hold you close.
      Then on the windy street you said goodbye
      and awkwardly fished from your pocket
      a gift, a bright pink yoyo.
      I see us in the streetlight, fingers touching briefly.

We are still nearly children ourselves,
and if I could, I would tell myself, Be proud,
and I would tell you, Be at peace.
Or maybe it should be the other way around,
because I was proud, I got to carry the ark,
shelter the light, you had to eat the bitter bread.

Since your card I've thought of you
and of our daughter,
my familiar all these years—
how she rides my life like a shut wing
on the small waves of my breathing
how the space for her remains
though redbuds shed their rubies—
yet the more I speak
the more I am helpless to answer.
Do you know how the curve of two arms reaching goes on and on?

I walked with my husband in the cold March night
where Orion and the Dipper shared the icy sky
and I thought of Indra's net, how one least touch
resonates and shimmers
through the crystal-starred, river-woven
infinite web of the world.
Then my sorrow ached like a knit bone
because it was such comfort that you grieve for her.

# Dent de Broc

*Dîtes-moi où, n'en quel pays. . . .*
—François Villon

I am Claude
I am bending over a fish
who swims beneath the ice
this water that holds me on its plate
while the crows shuffle their black cards
and the stars spin
The night my mother died she said
Claude, Claude, think of paradise
and when my father returns, bearing the
rabbit, fur and blood
on his rust-stained jacket
I will know that snow-starved look so well

If you come to the *Lion d'Or* you will see me
When I lie in my bed the earth spins
like fire
like the miller's daughter's hair

I will never marry unless my mother take me by the hand

2

I look at you and look at you
wondering what it is you are trying to say
I am Anne

I prayed to be burned because then God would speak to me
split heart, the yolk of lilies

burning glass to put out all the lights in all the windows

Though the women call me now to help with the fires I do not join them
I lie in my bed and dream of winter, dream of the crows

in the terrible branches

21

dream my newborn daughter
with the blue vein at her temples has died

Barefoot I search the snow for her
the pond the fires
                the mountain fields
search everywhere, so great is my fear

When I wake
I find on my pillow
a lump of coal and a sprig of red clover

# Liège, First Year, First Marriage

When my first husband was young
he had such beautiful knees: long, proud, symmetrical knees,
as at Mycenae in July
when we climbed the blazing hill
where Agamemnon, doomed, entered the lion gates.
At rugby that autumn he ran with the pack, lifting those knees
and flaring his nostrils, grimacing
around his mouth guard;
even when the ground was frozen and I stamped,
one foot, then the other,
hours together to keep warm, I watched,
how I watched, on that Belgian field
where the game calls hung sharp
on the air in Wallon and I spoke to no one.

Oh when he was young he palmed the world
like a basketball;
I was his, everything was his.
Days he practiced at the gym,
I stayed home, sat by the window,
my feet on the one bar heater
of our studio walkup above the *Quai de Rôme*
where coal barges plied the Meuse, heaped, nearly foundering;
where bargewives swept decks and hung out clothes
while their men steered the black weight north, beyond my vision:
past Liège; past slagheaps; through sooty towns
with *crachoirs* on the doorsteps,
starched lace curtains, sansevierias
at every window; along fields of trampled mud
lined with pollard sycamores;
past seagulls come inland
diving for refuse, screaming on the wind;
at last to Rotterdam, Maassluis, freighters—& the salt-stung open sea.

# Muerto, 1982

When you're packing, fixing to leave,
the junk drawer gets you. How can you say goodbye
to the chipped quartzite geode Megan gave you
before she was sent to the Menninger Clinic—
or the rusty sign stamped *AGRICULTURE*
you and Allan stole
from the tackroom of Littlejohn's stables?
Not to mention the matchbooks
from endless roadside restaurants,
a greasy tattered recipe card for crawfish
*étouffée*. And the glossy nighttime postcard
in its aqua Walmart frame,
the arc of lights spelling *CAVE LAND MOTEL*
all lit up like a Christmas tree
above *CHECK OUR PRICES DON'T BE MIS-LED*,
how can you leave this card
to the abuse and careless fingerings
of strangers? All the flotsam of your past,
junked in a kitchen drawer
in this narrow musty avocado townhouse
where you've tried to pretend
you're not desolate, not in the wrong marriage:
pack it in boxes and bags, it wants you,
everything you've ever done wants you to caress it,
and the deadweight lump of lead embossed with a pug dog
that you bought for a dollar
one rainy lonesome day on a back street in Virginia,
this relic wants you too. And the *muerto,* better take that,
better cherish the skeleton bride and groom
posed in their wooden matchbox,
in the background the crude outlines
of a tiny white cathedral, better wrap the *muerto*
and carry it to the yellow convertible
carefully, as if it were a robin's egg,

because if you are lucky
the man whose name's your secret,
the man who dreamed he could fly
the first time you slept beside him
and who waits for you now in the convertible,
tipping his face to the sun, as you shut the door
on the empty house
and enter the blinding April daylight,
if you are luckier than lucky
on some far, unimaginable afternoon or morning

this man will close your eyes—

II

# Daughters

My house is full of blood.
And my daughters, now,
who used to be so cleanly
cleft, so simple, carry
the bit flesh in them,
shark-torn fish trailing
blood in the sea. Even
my tortoiseshell, delicate,
female, yowls when the
blood comes to her, and,
tail up in anguish,
drags her pretty belly
on the ground.

My house is full of breasts,
softly deep and nippling
beneath camisoles or
sweaters. I have to inch
around them. I have to
squeeze by, narrow. They
float above my daughters
in the bathtub, I mean, they
*are* my daughters' in the
bathtub, pale, warm moons
in a watery sky, they who
suckled me now outdo me.

And though I do not stare,
my house is full of fur.
Already, boys
have touched it.
This, one daughter
tells me, and I think of how,
when she was born,

I stroked her arm so gently,
cherishing the vein-fine
skin, and swore no one would
ever hurt her.

# Mapplethorpe

So here I am the mom in the poetry class
and all week long the only photograph that really grabs me,
transfixes me, is the Mapplethorpe
erection I saw by accident once
at the bookstore across from the courthouse
as I browsed around downstairs while my husband read biographies
and the kids hunkered down with the joke books,
photograph of a cock so achingly huge
that whoever it was had laid it for mercy flat out on a table,
and it seems funny, all that braggadocio—women never understand
circle jerks, for instance, or teenagers measuring hardons;
imagine preparing yourself to lay yourself out
on the ironing board, your brickbat, little billyclub,
so here's this emptiness, I imagine a room
seven stories above the city, and in the other rooms
a bed with sheets that smell of Brut, a mildly leaky toilet
seeping into the mottled brown linoleum, kitchen
with dishes for three, stale ice, grease ring in the sink,
the doors are made of plywood, and these guys
who want to fill the time with their own heat
while the dust motes float in the chilly daylight,
one has the camera, the other
has his hand, and when it's ready he lifts his hand away
with such pride: quick, take it, you've got it,
nearly hovering above the earth, no before or after,
like angels turning the air to fire
with the slow rush of their wings;
secrets, how you want them, secrets of a closed room
high above the city, and the moment coming from nowhere,
leading nowhere, all your ruffles and feathers forfeit,
yourself shamed, proud, seen, yourself nothing but the parts
to worship you by, yes, I can understand it.

# Burning

"It's natural," my mother said, "It's so you can be a woman."
But shame lurked in her love. She made me burn my pads,

and when the pads were wet the middle didn't burn.
So I waited till the hall and kitchen were empty,

scurried downstairs from the fireplace,
and hid the blackened lumps, the charred rank blood, in the garbage.

I slipped past the door where my father lay in bed
all that cold rainy September, October,

or sat in an armchair swaddled in the buffalo plaid lap robe
that kept, years after, his smell, that I'd bring up close to my face

to breathe him in. My sister practiced Bach.
*Komm süsser Tod,* she wrote in her mottled notebook:

*Komm süsser Tod,* for I grow weary of my living. . . .
And my boyfriend strained against me

in cars, fields, borrowed rooms, until the tight flesh opened.
He laid me down and laid me down till I burned and begged,

"Could we take a walk, could we go to a movie?"
And I did my homework or painted my nails, a round-faced creature.

Then the spider chrysanthemums my father had saved,
chopping and burning savage-thorned blackberry creepers,

hauling railroad ties, shoveling dirt, all one August
terracing the whole matted, tangled, weed-choked hill

of a backyard singlehanded—the spider chrysanthemums
my father had saved, separating out the long, bedraggled,

all-but-smothered stems that I loved best of flowers
because they grew wild and spilled like white curved

feathers of seabirds across the rainsoaked earth
of the backyard's next-to-bottom terrace. . . . Such a struggle against cold:

my father dying, my mother grieving, my sister tranced,
my boyfriend gaunt and drenched, climbing the balcony railings

to knock on my window. And myself in that big white house
those silent hours: crouching, watching how the pads would open out

petal after petal, their rich earth salt smell peel, layer after layer.
I could poke them with the fireplace tongs, layers peeling. One would catch

fire, then the next, first the toilet paper swaddling, then the edges, last
the blood lump, hot coal, glowing, wet, stinking, not stinking.

Admit it, I liked the smell of my blood.

# Fugue

You ask me how I feel
about having a woman's body

And I think of Bach whom I love, whose music
reminds me of a high empty church,
airy, cold, a winter church, no an autumn church
because not so cold that you can't
get lost in your thoughts, Bach in flight
from his 20 children, blissed out, cold ecstasy,
and the purling brooks and rivers of music
that tumbled precise from his lofty passion—
nothing out of place, but all plenitude,
the pure impersonal

The closer I get to death the more I treasure
that serenity or ecstasy which is not love,
that going alone into it, like the silence
my mother lives with, my mother whose breasts
are as beautiful at 83
as the breasts of a 40-year-old woman. My mother
who lives alone still, whose wit is sharp and clear.
Whose favorite sound in nature
is a fast-running brook, a *bach,*
tumbling water down the creekbeds in Wyoming

Like those summers—1915, 1920—
when she lay at noon in the tent, watching light
come through the canvas
while she listened to the brook,
or woke in the morning when frost rimed the grass,
and ran from the tent, her footprints through the frost,
to plunge her face in the clear rushing water.

# The Heirlooms

We have come
to divide the inheritance.

She gestures once again
toward the Meissen porcelain fishing net
oozing eels, mackerel, and two fat babies,
the net held by two naked ladies, hair coiffed
and trailing, nipples tinged like coral,
seaweed draped across their ample ivory bodies.
Again she tells us how when we were small
we called the babies Ann and Jennifer . . . the girl Joan,
bending over . . . the largest pretty one Mama.

We make lists of our favorite things
but nobody wants the fishing net
though she tells us, too, how the Germans
brought their heirlooms to her door,
she paid *top price* in commissary rations,
gave them food that second winter
after war. Anna whose husband
had vanished. A child who brought one cup,
one plate to sell for bread. A Lutheran pastor
cradling, one hand in the other,
his ten Nazi-shattered fingers.

Still we do not want the fishing net
though she tells us, too, how Jennifer
and I, one 1950's evening,
announced at dinner to the Captains and their wives
that we were the babies, Joan and Mama
the pretty naked ladies, and Joan crimsoned
over, nipples—hers—implied.

Oh we are bad daughters
of such a mother, we are longing for our men,
for sex, gin-and-tonics, and our mother
wants to hold us once again—to make it go away,
our father's death and her crippled hip,
blotches of rosacea that cover her cheeks
and forehead, tears that won't stop seeping
from her eyes.

Now she creeps about the house,
giving it all away: pearl-handled fishknives,
demitasse cups and spoons, tea sets, trays,
and compotes—wrapped in Saran Wrap and stashed
in the freezer. On shelves, Bohemian crystal glasses
like emeralds and rubies, the cobalt-blue chocolate cup,
Spode figurines of birds and roses, Hummel,
Limoges, *Weintrauben* dishes with wreaths of green leaves.
Then she lowers herself infinitely slowly
into a dining room chair, lifts one arm
toward the porcelain fishing net, says,
Well maybe you'll call me ghoulish, but if you cremate me
you can put the nymphs and tritons in my arms.

I think I will break without her.

                              Put *her* in *their* arms,
my sister whispers, and I know she's trying
to comfort the same terror, trying to see our mother
borne out to sea in a net of love.

# Stroke

Still, her hands are beautiful, their veins
and crooked fingers
frail, with bones like sparrows'.
And the nails of her hands—
almond tapers, half moons—
they and the powerful cheekbones all that remains.

*

She slept on the eggcrate mattress
that brilliant afternoon.
I wished I could hold the pillow down,
she could be through then—
curled, unconscious,
her hair in tufts like feathers.

*

Kwan-non, her crystal statue,
Infinite Compassion,
rides in the sea of her azure bowl,
which is smooth within,
lightly scaled outside,
like fishes in the Milky Way.
Kwan-non will come to me,
the bowl to Jennifer,
and I will stroke the crystal
which flows
and floats. . . .

# At Azalea Gardens

Then there is just the brute sledgehammer blow of missing you.

Like tonight at the library, passing the shelf
with the Large Print mysteries, living once again
how I took you books at Azalea Gardens,
how it spun steadily downhill the year you lived there:
first your grand plans for what they called the Faulkner apartment
and your worries, would the residents like you
even if you rented the most expensive.
Then tea parties, mutual eyeings of treasures,
all the old lady wreaths and coasters
to make a home where there was none. Then your falls,
the day you got stuck hanging halfway out of your armchair,
emergency call button broken, how you balanced there two hours
until we got there. Then the dead weight of you,
trying to get you back to bed, wig skewed over your face,
and I thought dear God let her die this afternoon
in so much sunlight. Then the man who blew his nose
into his napkin, your rages, how you thought they were trying to steal from you.

The week before you left I drove out one night
and sat in the car, looking up at the Faulkner window
right at the center of Azalea Gardens, and mama I cried for an hour,
seeing your window was lighted and soon would not be.

# Her Silence

That day I entered her silence.
I wore it like a dress all afternoon, its brown
and turquoise folds sank down around me.
Forbidden as a child to kiss her lips,
I leaned over her then and kissed her lips.
At first I couldn't
touch her mouth with mine, I brushed the air
where sour breath rose from the pit of broken teeth,
the perishing organs that labor within her—
but then I kissed her, felt the cool
papery skin, put my hand on the pulse
of her neck, plump and almost unbearably soft,
and became for an instant my father,
home from the war
fifty years ago, bent over her, adoring.

                  I neared the house today
after long rain, slowing to take the muddy curve,
thinking of her in her bed again.
A yellow-shafted flicker, fire patch flicking,
strutted bold as you please in the yard with cats.
Birds sang with strong sudden joy in the privet—
mockingbirds, cardinals, raucous jays.
I held wishes on my tongue, drank air as deeply
as years. Mother, never far from me, or near,
even in dreams I listen for questions that gather
unspoken. *Who are you?*
*Are you chilly? Are you chilly?* That day
I gazed like a newborn into her milky eyes,
hung speechless on her breath,
as love lifted through me like birdsong.

# Mother  Mother  Mother  Mother  Mother

1

Brown Melmac on the table wouldn't break—
dishes for 1950s families—
but knife scars mapped them, tracks
of the endless meat loaf, ham steaks,
peas from the freezer, rice, and mashed potatoes.
Spode was for good, scooped and scalloped
with scarlet roses. "Girls, we have beautiful things,"
our mother told us. She collected from two wars,
scouting the antique stores of the Occupied nations.
But at least she paid top dollar
when the Germans brought their heirlooms to the door
for hand-me-down wool, for butter and bacon.
We clung to her skirts like burrs
after we moved to Pennsylvania,
in the side yard with two birch trees
we played duck, duck, goose or ring around a rosy,
and when she slipped inside
we'd follow a moment later,
thumbs in our mouths, stricken at her vanishing.

2

I don't know who invented Let's Describe,
but we played it constantly.
She was herself, no one more splendid: Mrs. Welpton;
we were Mrs. Jones and Mrs. Bell.
Trained to share our cookies even-Steven,
one had one more emerald, the other, one more ruby.
We had houses with twenty-five bedrooms,
yachts in our private harbors, always
a penthouse ballroom, and the clothes—
fur coats for Mrs. Welpton; for us, peignoirs, chiffon—
in coral, aqua, seafoam. . . . And the paper dolls
she drew us, one foot pointing downward,
the other arching sideways. . . . "Draw the bodice,"
I once told her, wanting that double U penned in,
bosoms cupping like Wonder Woman's,
like Ronnie's mother's at Sunday School. "I'm glad
you're older," I once told her. But I wished
she had sexy blonde hair, a mole,
and stick-out breasts like twin torpedoes.

3

No cussing, no drinking, no sex before marriage,
but iceberg lettuce with too much salt.
Hymns hummed at the ironing board,
Toni perms, and organdie dresses.
Sometimes she drove you mad—her "Mabel, Mabel,
sweet and able, keep your elbows
off the table," her ribbons and gloves
for little ladies. Anger was not allowed,
rough craziness was not allowed,
sickness and death were not allowed.
Christian Science usurped our bodies. "I'm six today,"
a girl lisped once in Sunday school,
and my mother's friend the teacher replied, "No, darling,
you are the perfect child of God." "No, I'm six
today," the girl insisted. "No you're not,
darling, you couldn't be, God made you
his perfect child." I listened, mortified: *Six, teacher, six.* . . .

4

Birth
and the savage adoration of bodies, child for mother, mother for child:
my head in her lap, I'd listen to her stomach rumble
and smell her sometimes woman smell.
Unthinkable, I the raw birth eel
squeezed bloody out of her body.
The sweat on her laboring face and neck,
taut cords, convulsing belly. . . .
Not for us even the slightest clue of her cries, her pain—
or joy, the way she turned to my father—
But her armpit was my nesting place,
the knob on her wrist my fascination.
Once, she had a thigh-high bruise
from banging into a standing ashtray. Her voice
was low, she overcooked broccoli, she was my queen.
And last spring, the last word she will probably
ever say to me?—finally, after days by her bed,
a glimmer crossed her brain
and she smiled, the smile got stuck,
she grinned and beamed like a baby, five minutes;
looking straight at me, she whispered, "*Sweetheart*". . . .

# Wedding *Obi*

Kyoto in 1955
    the market of shifting silks, that rainy Easter after war,
when we walked along the alley where the fingernail weaver
    crouched above his loom and wove the wedding *obi's*
                           chrysanthemums and cranes,
cherry blossoms, swirling water, pine tufts with crooked branches,
    gold
        and crimson leaves

and the man whom my mother called my father
gazed at her, leaning slightly over her as she bent to touch the *obi*,
    she in her soft black coat, he so dignified and stiff
                            in his Army uniform,
stranger newly back from three years' war.

I knew for certain that man was not my father.
My mother slept with him, she wore his pearls and garnets,
    but I became convinced, one night on the ship
                         as I tossed in my bunk
    on the voyage to Japan,
we were being led into treachery, spies had taken my father, he was
                         dying in chains
in a quonset hut outside Seoul.

Memory was shifting, beautiful, uncertain,
    like the alley where silk organza
                  shimmered and floated like wings
of every bird in paradise—
                    viridian, copper,
cobalt,
    pink like the tender, silken conch,
            pale daffodil, silver, vermilion—.
My father hid his face
    in that far-off land of quonset huts and spies,

and even she kept her secrets. I tagged along till my legs burned
    and cramped with growing pains,
                                but my mother never told me

how she knew this was the man she should lie down with.
                    For her he had not changed.
She just touched the wedding *obi*, lifting a corner
    a little toward me, and said, "See the pattern of seasons?
That's how the obi weaver
weaves eternity for marriage."

III

# The Day of the Dead

*—Morgue Series, Andres Serrano*

Three times I leave the room
and three times, shamefaced, I return
to the nine bright photographs,
each as big as a door: the bits of bodies.

                                 Serrano has draped
her eyes and brow with red, the woman
with nosehair and a moustache who looks like a man,
dead of infectious pneumonia. She is
beautiful, her fierce lips, the exact rough grain
of her pitted skin. . . .

                 And the little girl
who died of meningitis, her eyelashes
feather in abandonment
out from the lids, across her cheek;
soft wisps of light brown hair
lie across her slightly blotched
and slightly puffy forehead.

                       Watching these faces, I want
to go to the vanishing point
where the lines of the walls converge.

           What would the rat-poison suicide do,
punch away an intruder
with those kickboxing hands, the stubby nails chlorotic?
Serrano has covered her face with black,
she's wearing a white lace camisole . . . her skin has stiffened
with gooseflesh, the poison
starts from every pore of her body.

               And the black man's beautiful lips,
his dignity like stark, picked fields

in the Mississippi Delta; he doesn't look dead,
that one eloquent line curving down from the left top lip. . . .
Then the drowned woman, gray-brown, warts or moles on her chest,
a small cut on her shoulder.
She's pouting, all the river the mud, she's pouting.

                                  I can't look at the
burned—
So I turn to the knifed, two photos of her hands and wrists, visionary,
mute, with gashes like eyes.

And again and again, little girl, little girl. Two years old? Three?
           I want to stroke her forehead.
I want to kiss the black man's lips,
                 unclench the suicide's fingers.

                         To call to them all: Come away—

                 The voice takes me, tells me:
Bow down and be quiet before these images.
Of course you can look upon them.
They will just open you to a greater tenderness.

# What Is There to Do in Mississippi?

It's not about desire,
this land that pulls us in
and gets us lost on back roads
till we come to an impassable bridge
at midnight by some bayou.
Our headlights useless, we just
sit silent
where kudzu looms like velvet
to swath and choke the pines.
Crickets chirr. Spring peepers
clamber to crescendo in the waters.

Later, we touch. I hold your face in my hands
and my body comes alive
like those crickets in the kudzu.
But now we sit not touching in the car.
The singing night pours down around us.
Great splayed towering leaves
begin to teach us our oblivion.

# Ice Storm

In the ice storm Thursday half our trees came down.
Behind the house the forest exploded like popcorn.
We stood by the window watching branches burst and shatter,
tortured by the ice that hurtled down like daggers
from the goddess whose fingers are talons,
whose skirt is knives.
At three a.m. the big one—the hundred-year-old magnolia tree.
The meterbox ripped away, line down, a terrific shudder
of glass and wood, the whole house shook.
Now branches hang crazy, by threads—
willow oaks and pecan trees,
shards of heartwood broken radii and ulnas
jutting into the leadwhite sky
like beggars in a badly acted stageplay
who thrust up stumps, beseeching heaven,
hurling imprecations. But no, the trees submit;
it's only we who cower. The cats are more like us,
they streaked out of the forest to the house
and spent the next day spraying—hats, gloves, doorjambs—
stinky gusts of Here I am, don't mess with my place.
We're like that. Anxious. Fretful. Squabbling.
Anything but silent.
Yet hardest to tell, the knowledge
that we had been given a gift. Not just that we came through
safe, but that, for a few moments
at dawn the second day,
the storm still raging, the forest shining,
branches flying like bullets, like angels,
ourselves beyond fear into rapt calm,
we touched the hem of a final morning.

Now debris, downed lines, no water.
Snarl and tangle of branches interflung, wall-to-wall
disaster. Start here little ants, sort your peas and lentils,
twigs and branches by the curb, chop, saw the big ones,
somewhere under there's
the world as you once knew it: the rosebush, the crocuses.

# And from the East
## Like a Long Coffin Being Drawn

*after a William Eggleston photograph*

The weavings catch the light:
the gypsy moths have spun their luminous messes.
Sweet on the air as muscadines, kudzu roils
and flows, and chokes the valley. It's August.
Headed homeward, I slough through dust and gravel

and think of the photograph, the convict,
he leads the mules along sun-battered cottonfields.
Dust drifts around them, him and his companion
in cap and shirt or jacket. Westward they plod, across
the grainy paper. Dust sifts up around the bellies of the mules.

His left arm hangs, hand across his thigh, somehow
it holds his shoulders up. His head bows, with that proud,
stiff, desolate young man's bow.

The men don't talk; they're there.
Two men, six mules, heading into dust. He's riding,
leading his partner. Their faces are turned away from me.

# Eddie

*We have no sense of the history of children.*
—Robert Moses

He was twelve
and big for his age,
one of those beautiful children
whose thickening muscles and long, heavy bones
promise them early to manhood.
When I read to the children
in Miss Gardiner's fifth grade,
he'd curl up on the beanbag by my feet
or lean against my arm to see the pages.
Until Brooke and JoAnne, one morning,
suddenly prickling up,
made cootie-brushing motions
and said "Eww Eddie, get lost,
don't touch us." Maybe you'd say
they were just like girls everywhere,
and who can fault them their fierce bonding.
But they were white
and this was Mississippi.
He fell to the floor as if shot
and began to cry. When I put my hand on his shoulder,
he went rigid and hard as wood,
flipped like a fish and set his back against me.

# Shorty

Under the neighbor's plum tree,
Shorty, dum-de-dum casual, drops fruit
into a grocery bag. Or slips up from the garden,
knobs beneath his shirt,
one hand waving vaguely as if shooing flies before him.
Tells me, "These be green. I was jus
walkin through, I was thinkin I be checkin on yo tomatoes."
Tells me where he lives:
"Shack behin Isaiah Busy Bee Cafe
on that hillside down by Kroga." On his kudzu-swaddled porch,
a blue sprung chair. From cut-down milk
bottles and rusted gallon cans, scraggly stalks of geraniums
spring, and salvia, splotched coleus,
red clover.

When his shack burns, what does he live on,
where does he sleep?—Bandy-legged, bright in a handmedown
lilac-turquoise-black-plaid shirt, he trails
a rusty mower door to door.
Next year I pass him by chance, in Baptist Memorial to visit a baby.
Sweat-slick on a high white bed,
he clutches his stomach
and says, "They cuttin on me."

Trickster, spirit of place. . . .

He vanishes, appears; vanishes, appears,
at the mouth of a steaming woods.
Grizzled, knob-kneed, like a holograph
or smoke, he turns his hands out,
turns his hands out:
his leaf-green hospital gown
in shreds beneath a torn plum-purple blazer.
Trumpetvine snakes to the edge of the sky.
Great red branches bend down to him like fever.

# Letter from Oxford, Mississippi

Home again, I sink in this wet air.
The ceiling fan stirs the same thick juices
of summer. My garden, grown rank in daily rain,
sprawls and rots, this steaming August.
Eggplants and peppers fester. Marigolds blacken.
The sun, where the worm has eaten,
splits and gouges my tomatoes. Black and yellow,
mildew blossoms in the drainboards.

Beautiful, big as my thumb,
pincer-tipped legs cradling her gauzy egg sac,
web with its zigzag Jacob's ladder
stretching to fill my kitchen window,
the spider starves,
waits.

*

Something wants me to sleep, to sink
heavy into the bonedrowse of summer, wants me to
live in this place and not tell its story . . .
to roll my window up, ignore the swollen stench
of roadkill on the road, putrefaction
thick and sweet, swaddled by kudzu in ditches . . .
to forget what I have driven by
and dreamed: mud, earthsprawl, tangle
of thicket, they led the three men out
where night boiled with cicadas;
they had dug the earthen dam
for Schwerner, Chaney, Goodman
near the fairgrounds in Neshoba—

and Jordan, left guarding the entrance,
came running, shouting, "Save one for me!"
and Chaney, the black man,

was last to die, and Jordan, wiping his gun
on his pants, said, "You didn't leave me
nothing but a nigger, but at least
I got a nigger."

*

I want to tell you.

Seven white men
have taken Henry Lowry
from Sardis, Mississippi
to Wilson, Arkansas.
It is 1921. *En route*
they stop for lunch.
(Do they chat with the
reporter? He
writes *in medias res:*
"Nothing has occurred
to mar the serenity
of the party's  journey.")
It is January. The vines
have no leaves, the unpicked
bolls of cotton hang
from brittle stalks, the
ground perhaps has frozen.
With the Mississippi
on one side and a huge lake
on the other, five hundred
people watch him as,
lit by small leaves and
gasoline, once or twice
he tries to reach and eat
hot coals to die
faster as flesh drops
from his legs but they
kick the coals away and
then when the flames lick
his abdomen two men begin

58

to question him, Yes, he says,
Yes he killed the man who owned
the farm where he was tenant,
Yes he killed the daughter.
Among those in
the crowd are Lowry's wife
and children. Words fail
to describe—the second
reporter notes—words fail
to describe the sufferings
of this man. He burns
for forty minutes, care-
fully ignited, inch
by inch. Only once
does he cry out.

The townsfolk came
to "converse" with him
while the white men
ate that leisurely lunch.
And he was all alone.

Nerve end
by nerve end.
Minute by minute.

*

I walk past the jail near my house.
Black men lean on the chainlink fence,
too hot and listless for trouble.
Bone-heavy with death, all you can think in the summer is
this land wants to climb on me and kill me.
And again and again, when I drive up the road
past the gully, I see the ghost,
Joe Christmas, hands manacled, running
and dodging through the kudzu, through the snakes
and briars, the wet thick lethal Mississippi August.
Fatherless, fugitive, he runs and feints

toward his only hope, the defrocked man of God,
only to discover that he has
already failed him. Done damned in Jefferson, I tell you,
and as we shuffle through these streets
where sun blisters the tar
till it smells of sweet sharp sin
and shines likes the wings
of the fallen angels,
we know it.

# Sweetgum Country

Billy shows us his arm, burned by the sun
where pesticides sensitized his skin
those years of his childhood, playing
in Delta cotton fields. A charred,
hand-sized lozenge marks the tender crease
inside his elbow. Alex holds up her chart
that shows the sickness and death
in her mother's family, from cancer
in Cancer Alley. She has made red circles
for "fought," green crosses for "died,"
she has put stars around her name,
my pretty dark-haired student.
They come to class, my sixteen freshmen,
and no matter what their topics,
they all say, "I never *knew* this. . . ."

Fords and Chevies that will barely crank
one more time are parked in the reeds
and slick red mud. Early evening sun
pours down on the cypresses and sweetgum,
the Tallahatchie swamp at the edge
of Marshall County. Turtles poke their heads up.
Cottonmouths zipper through the black water
or stretch out long and bask on the abandoned
railroad bridge. Men and women of all ages
beguile the hours after work,
the idle hours, with soft talk or silence,
with bamboo poles and battered coolers.
They could use the food.
They fish for buffalo, catfish, bass,
despite the fish advisories, the waters laced with mercury.

# Jitney Food Store

*for Lucille Clifton*

I pass the old brick jail
where black men used to press
against the chainlink fence,
where weeds craze the macadam
and the basketball hoop
still hangs by a thread
for the slow lope of prisoners.

I pass the Jitney food store
and nearly collide with an
exiting man, his eyes
fathomless . . . hostile . . . sleepy.
I'm shamed by his hasty sidestep,
one thigh up to guard his crotch
from my eager dog—sunken
crotch, in dead brown pants,
and dog we found abandoned,
starving in the woods,
who sometimes snarls at men, at
black men—

I yank him tight on chokehold.
Thank God this time
he doesn't snarl, I don't
have to grin that shiteater's grin,
sorry sir, it's the dog, not me.
But everywhere
the history of our history.

# At the Beginning of the Century
# It All Seems Nearly Over Already

Through Alabama that afternoon and into Mississippi—

Tuscaloosa to Gordo, Columbus to Okolona,
then on up to Pontotoc—all we passed was clearcut
clearcut: red clay hills, eroded gullies, trash timber

piled by the sides of the road—then a car that had swerved
and crashed on the sudden curves near Gordo
(how many folks in that battered, filthy Chevy?)

and a small child on a blanket, ashen and unmoving,
a woman stroking its hair, staring off into the pine trees,
skinny men and children clustered in the ditch,

a man directing traffic, his blaze orange cap and belly—
then ambulance, firetrucks, sheriff—then later
a hand-painted sign nailed to a scrawny sweetgum:

*Even So Lord Jesus Come The Day Is Evil*

# Raccoons, A History

We watched him last summer by flashlight,
moonlight, sharp paws flickering,
thick-furred body anxious and upright—
*Quick, quick,* he'd dive at the cat food,
then feint and check for danger. Now it's January,
raining, death swells in the walls—
he must have come home to die last fall,
slunk off into the crawl space.
First we noticed the sweetness,
the something-not-quite-clean-here.
Was it a squirrel, a mouse? we wondered.
Weeks passed, and it didn't diminish—
Could we take the boards off? No, too old,
they would splinter. And we didn't know
for certain where the dead thing was.
So my husband climbed on to the roof
to shovel ten pounds of quicklime into the crawl space—
and found the other raccoon, the little female.
Shivering and scrawny,
she tried to squeeze into the hole
but he blocked it with the quicklime.
He said, "She looked sad. She turned away."

Las spring they were born in the walls,
where my daughter slept in the guest room bed.
We heard them scrabbling, squeaking.
"It's beasts," I said, "are they dying?"
But she laughed like she laughed when she was little—
"Mom, listen to them, they're snuggling, they're happy."
They grew and climbed out from the roof,
played with their mother and dug through the compost,
pawed at the screen on the kitchen window.
We loved them. Then the big one
started to fight the female, scratching and snarling.

Plenty of food for both of them,
but he'd snap and slash till she cowered on the deck
with her one filched piece of cat food.

Sometime in the fall, the mother vanished.
For the big one and the female, was it sickness? Poison?

—January, raining, first came the stench,
then quicklime dusting down from between the beaded boards,
then snow, and the smell diminished.
Now lime-floured flies
drawn forth by the warmth of the kitchen
dot the walls, caress the light globes, circle and hover like ghosts, stunned.
I vacuum them up, they're easy targets,
but wave after wave they emerge from the door jamb.

# Where, Beneath the Magnolia

*for Teresa Washington*

Wind shakes
the shabby cedars,
gusts and torments blowing up
harder and harder
over the mosses of Rowan Oak—
where the brick-laid maze,
derelict now, beautiful
circled the ancient magnolia,
eaten and hollowed
and finally last year
storm-stricken,
now only a pile of black shards
and leafmeal—where once
Teresa stood
in sweat-shimmering August
in a bower of whispering
branches,
and spoke with Caroline Barr
in tongues and rattles
and honeyed
groanings. Fern-furred
branches bowed
above the burnished
river their voices
conjured,
Teresa deep
in her Ifá trance
speaking with Caroline,
dead since 1940—with the woman
behind the book,
the woman
behind the word,
whom Teresa, unafraid,
could spell

from the monstrous
shadows. Tongues
and echoes, blue buzzings
in the honeysuckle,
snail-shine and humus
beneath them . . . bracken,
bloodroot, mutterings
in the air—they spoke
and were not
as they'd been spoken.
How can I say
what passed between them
in the rising wind?
What blossoms
has no name.

IV

# Reiki

*(after September 11)*

So many souls like white petals
flung in the ashen dawn of the 21$^{st}$ century.
Rain wets the oaks, washes the dusty privet—
down falls rain, down fall the spiraling leaves,
but flutesong rises and cloud-smoke rises,
I watch it outside the darkening window;
the circles around you are whole and beautiful,
and why fear death
while late October light is turning and turning.

*

Here are my hands—love's conduit in a small house
through simple curving flesh, the momentary architecture
of bone. You this hour's beloved could be anybody,
you and I scarcely persons, but warmth and emptiness,
and the trance that stills and fills my hands
no more mine than the wind
that swells the wet oak leaves outside the window.
Yes outside this place we are afraid.
But here let you rest yourself easy.

Let my hands like sleep still the fluttering of your eyes

and at your head's crown let them sink
against hair springing soft and thick
from your salty scalp, day's sweat damp beneath my fingers

then over your cheeks and ears let them shelter you
tender as sassafras leaves that hang lobed and moist
along the trails down by the river

let them bless the wings of your shoulders

and the flowering light
at throat     heart     gut
the pulse and lymph where groin meets thigh

Now as you lie on your belly
let my hands rest on the taut arching ribs—
heart's cage—the honeycomb of lungs, then lower let them

hover above the dark knobs of kidneys

and cup the root chakra     clean     impersonal
five fingers rest on the base of your spine
five fingers cup the thick curve of your buttocks

let my hands breathe with your breathing, rise and fall
as rain falls     as flute music
rises and falls in a distant room

deeper than sleep you are lulled and loved     there now     there

the ark of your flesh     floating now     upon still waters

# Limen

*Now the souls gathered. . . .*
—Book XI, The Odyssey

Red berry of my heart
be the blood these shadows seek.

Where the tooth-edged dogwood blossoms
at the threshold of the pines

lie down among tall grasses.

Let the slow rains pearl your hair
let your snail skin grow translucent

and your throat's soft chirring flow
in the twilight's white-tongued river.

# Of

Poetry is of the soul but when the soul is tired and full of grief
the hands must continue to live
honorably,
feeling the dog's thick ruff or the tender crease of his armpits
for plump summer ticks, plucking them, creasing them
between fingernails, and then the blood spurt.

Poetry is of the hands, how they caress and care
for the hot, itch-plagued animal,
while the soul
wanders vacant all day long
where bald cypresses grip down in muck,
loom up through the snakethick, shadowfevered river.

# How Death Came to the Horse

*Guanacaste, Costa Rica*

It came to her in the long field
near men with purple shirts and callused hands
who did not see, men who raised amber glasses
or turned from the table to spit
*semillas de las sandías* into the dust
while *salsa* blared through static on the patio.
It came to her while the battered handmedown bus
brilliant with hummingbirds, rainbows, toucans
in painted paradise, ground up the rutted hill
to Monteverde. Tourists and *ticos* did not see
how it came to her while milch cows
and one lone Brahma bull, its hump
the shadowy brown of dust and honey,
grazed, swinging their heavy heads
near cattle egrets that thronged low spreading trees
like linen hung to dry, like hunchbacked angels.
But it singled her out and she accepted it,
lay down beneath the sun,
put her legs out stiff and straight
while men drank or laughed or spat out seeds.

# Waking

Waking
         this first morning
                     after the bitter
                 rain washed mud
into a gash of grave
             where your mother
                         and your father
                     oh, what—
waited?
             shifted their long
                         brown bones?
                 or nothing?
Only the heart
             wants them
                         still to want him,
                 your brother
laid yesterday
             by his last wish
                         beside them—
                 in a rough pine box
in the freezing rain.

                 ***

             Smoke seeps
                     from a newcut
                 grave. Three foxes
appear, muzzles high,
             sniffing
                         the thin blown snow,
                 head toward the
brambly, luminous
             woods—not a dream,
                         quite, but a gift,
                 as if something

loves us—
       and vanish away from me.
               Blessings
         upon the dead
vanishing lightly,
      wind in the brush
             of their tails. . . .
        But for you,
waking?
      I hold you,
             flesh heavy
       with sorrow.

# Light. Olympic Valley, California

*in memory of Zdenek Sirovy*

You bring your grief to the mountain. Lay it down.
The shaggy mules'-ears dance in this clear light
and the shadow of each long leaf joins in the dancing.

Blue lupine, speckled alyssum
sending off sugar and heat, the poppies' furling gold—

what do they know of desolation? How could the ragged daisies
stop plunging in the wind,
or dust and day relinquish their bright unfolding?

The pine mat manzanita, low mariposa lily,
a junco's click and trill,

or that skinny brown horse in the stableyard,
one ear cocked,
softly whickering, shifting his haunches,

and all the light you will ever need.

# Pleasures of the Text

## 1  The Favorite Words of Albert Camus

*le monde*

      Blood oranges, cut

    *la douleur*

        on a blue

        *la terre*

          glass plate.

*la mère*

      White candles.

    *les hommes*

        What of it?

      *le désert*

         Lilies. Lilies.

*l'honneur*

      You turn away

    *la misère*

        into the sun.

      *l'été*

         A strip of sand where
         Marie in green
         smiles back
         on the arm
         of another man
         already.

     *la mer.*

## 2 Mermaid, Singing

Oh T. S. Eliot, I put my head down on the desk
the morning Jacqueline White,
11th grade honors English,

told us you had died.
I was pushing out breasts as fast as I could,

studying my French, haunting the foreign movies.
One day soon I would pack my bags
and fly to England.

In my black turtleneck, ankh necklace,
fishnet stockings, I would arrive at your door.

Loneliest man in the world,
I sketched a charcoal of your face
and could not sleep without it near—

## 3  After a Death

I read in a dexedrine haze,
rocking my body
until everything turned white.

> Vladimir: You don't know if you're unhappy or not?
> Boy: No Sir.
> Vladimir: You're as bad as myself.

The rainbirds
came alive each dawn.

All that spring,
after my first child's death,
words carried me.

4  *Les vrais paradis sont les paradis qu'on a perdus*


Stop a little, child, look from the window.
Do you see chestnut trees lifting their candles,
the draft horse that pulls the milk wagon
still in his traces? The pond is so quiet.
Ducks have settled for the night, the soft brown wives,
the arrogant papa with his curling tailfeather.
They sleep by those willows
with their heads beneath their wings. Look, the last rays
of the sun—like a conflagration,
that flock of pigeons rising from the steeple.
How the souls hurry on, without hope of paradise.

You become so big, you're up to my heart already.

## 5 *Delicious relations*

Take this whole
day: tuberous begonia
shell-pink fleshy hairy on the old broken
bench the pecan
so full of nuts its branches touch
the ground moist grasses scintillant
dew flashing and dog
frisky gallumphing feathery
tail bobbing old
yellow tennis ball slobbery
big flappy lips hanging down.
Then the tortoiseshell's
riding my husband's
back in the sunlight
spills through our
window she gnaws my wrist I bite
his ear high school
band practices   Brrrumm oompah
he says mmm I love this
October   music floats through the forest
up the valley.

## 6  Negative Capability

Here I am, maundering about the house
in my nightgown
all this clear October morning,
thinking of Keats again. The light in me
greets the light in you. I want
to tell him that "To Autumn," where you see him
shut the door on that one rising note of agony,
and turn back to the world's
blossoming— Well, Frederick Mulhauser,
thirty years ago, never could teach that poem.
Most professorly, he would tilt his chair back,
prop his feet up, light his pipe, shuffle his papers,
speak, choke. Harumph. Harumph. His voice
would utterly fail him. "That boy. . . ."

The ability to become nothing—a gift
we all have, but
*to say* the brief, transitory shining. . . .

7  The Favorite Words of Albert Camus

The heart's jesses
                              *le monde*
        are loosed.
                                      *la douleur*
             Earth  unfolds
                                              *la terre*
her terrible bounty.
                          *la mère*
        And the man
                                  *les hommes*
                or woman
                                              *le désert*
of honor rejoices
                              *l'honneur*
             though suffering
                                      *la misère*
                bears shoreward
                                              *l'été*
with every beat
                          *la mer*
        of the sea.

V

# Open Like a Rose

"Open like a rose," he told me,
"open like an orchid,"
chanting all the names of flowers he knew

while I pushed and two nurses held my knees:
"open like a bird of paradise, open
like a daffodil, a tulip,

a magnolia, a hollyhock, a marigold."
I laughed—this endless list,
and the stubby, stinking marigold—

and something fiery opened,
ring upon ring. *With my body I thee worship.*
All of it, I guess. All of my body, I mean,

but all of *it,* too: the violence, the boredom.
Once, he cracked my tooth; I nearly ran him over,
he was plastered to the windshield

yelling "Go ahead and do it."
Venus rises to the moon above the mountain,
and here, in the West, I miss lying in his arms

full of my usual doubts
about my wrinkles and my flesh,
full of my usual grief

that as fast as whiskers can push from his skin
or his balls pull up tight the way I love them,
he is going away from me,

I am going away from him,
one of us will close the other's eyes.
*With my body.* . . . The night we first made love

he had to leave me, dress,
ride out in the rain for rubbers.
When he returned, rain streaking the window

and that slippery blue sleeping bag
falling off the bed,
I held him so joyfully, both of us married elsewhere.

# Iraklion

We slept by day and wandered all night
past concrete shells like locust husks
thrown down fast for the tourist season.
We lay on stones that slicked the sea
and barely mentioned our pasts, our future.
Once, at dawn, we came to the market
and came to the butcher, where light
sprang from gristle, and the smeared flanks
of goats and sheep hung heavy, hooked,
and glistened. Lavalike, we flowed together;
our nostrils quickened with the sweet
of spoiling blood. Fire though there was not fire.
And bone, beak, hoof, tendon—
the man with the knives, his crimson apron.

# *Gala* / Milk

Now my nipples are quiet flowers,
late light-bent.
My shadow slides beneath my feet
and stretches mountainward.
Spent lupine, a scribble of grasses.

Five times, the milk blossomed through me.
Five times I stepped, holding my babies,
into that hot, starry river.

No more fingers
will hook into my mouth,
no more heads will butt me
like lambs to knock the milk down.

I cannot tell, tonight,
if I am frightened or full of praise.

# You Know This

That's the thing. You get the smell of defeat and the others start to circle around you, baring their teeth. Or they back away from you, afraid. And the more you smile and chat and try to keep up the old games, the more it doesn't work. You're like the person with the whip snapping at the circus diver, lashing him terrified out on the high dive, closer and closer to the edge. And you're the diver too, your toes cling for safety to the rough board, feeling land below you still, not the free fall toward what may or may not be water. Or you're a moose on an iced-over lake surrounded by wolves. You were enormous and strong once, weren't you?—now you're trying to keep up, trying to brazen it out, so your eyes don't show the bewilderment, the pleading. Thing is, there's not a person who's not afraid, just as you are. Who can't be turned on or left hung out to dry like the dishcloth that dried all the camping utensils, red checked cloth slung soggy and stained over a log.

Dear God I want to tell someone how on the way home I stopped in the sun and stood on the sidewalk watching a squirrel so close to me digging, digging, then running away worried, then approaching, perching, his tail twitching in beautiful ripples of warning, like water flung from a backdoor dishpan, ripples of shining, his chocolate-drop eyes fixing on me, his shoulders and muscled jaws quivering, then edging back toward me to dig some more. He was using his pointy little paws to fling the dirt out sideways, eating roots or blades of grass or whatever he found, and then finally, Eureka! he lifted it out, an ancient pecan, nearly as long as his face was wide, and he scampered off, jaws stretched around it, to the base of the oak tree. And I thought the same old thing people have thought forever. Lucky squirrel, he doesn't have to be human.

But how is it possible—you know this too, you do: How is it possible to reach adulthood, maturity, to see and think and feel for all these years, and not sometimes to feel as if you are carrying your life like a basket of eggs that you'd lay down?

# Happiness

The wind returns and we are still alive
this Mississippi morning.
You kick up your heels though nearly 50,

do a shimmy, a High-5 down the street.
"Ha! Can't beat me. Made it through another summer."
Later I walk the dog

down my favorite pebbled road beside the graveyard
past crimson sumac, goldenrod,
thickets where kudzu dangles,

sugar and sunlight like muscadine wine.
A shiny red flatbed truck
chugs by me up the hill, a young man driving,

a woman in the flatbed: calm, billowy.
Children all sizes of small
blossom like hollyhocks around her,

girls in cornrows
with orange, green, yellow, lilac barrettes,
bigger boys in red—

Where are they going? I wonder,
then think of a painting in Bern:
*It is a boat, he is carrying them to Paradise.*

She smiles, I wave. The children begin to chant
soberly, shyly,
"Hi doggie hi doggie hi doggie."

# The Blessing of My Beloved on My Body

I was lying on my side curled up like a snail
on our flannel-sheeted futon,
because I was ashamed

of my aging body, while outside the dogwoods
turned ragged in nearly November,
curling down their leaves like ballerinas' toes,

exposing hard scarlet berries; he snuggled down,
we were stoned, he burrowed in and licked my asshole,
hard to write it, he licked my asshole,

and for the first time in my life
it was just like all the rest of me,
its narrow folds its fissure just flesh;

I would not be anything other—
in this house all made of wood
surrounded by scruff of the autumn garden

beneath scudding winds, stormlight,
I would not have anything other than this life,
mossy scurf and froth

that furs the gnarled magnolia tree
in the yard next door outside my window
where two white siamese cats,

one licking its paw, curl up beneath the yellow plastic chairs
on the porch of the derelict mansion
where lived the Civil War colonel and statesman

Lucius Quintus Cincinnatus Lamar—
how have I come to live in Mississippi?
how have I come to be 48 years old

and still not the clear blue flame I wanted to be?
I keep wanting to tell you about this innocence,
and my children, if you read this, drop the attitude;

when I'm clean bones
beneath my granite plaque down the rainy hill,
you'll remember,

the warm mouth of my beloved
blessed me, the warm tongue of my beloved
licked me.

# Multiflora Roses

In slow heat the walls breathe.
Back and forth flies scutter at the window.
Objects dance with their dust

and in the mansions of the neighbors
nothing is ever lost: socks, chicken bones,
*Eagles* from twenty years ago. . . . What happens

if you leave it alone, let the house fill
with wornout skirts
and shoes, dark soles walked slick,

torn petticoats, stained nylon underwear?
If you let the trees go, stop watering,
turn aside into your own absentness

until spiders haunt the drifted leaves
and ivy slithers,
furred, abundant, to the tips of branches?

*

Caleb's discovered The Doors
and shouts the music we listened to once,
each separately. *Come on baby light my fire.* . . .

In his room with the ceiling fan
thunking out summer
he rocks and shakes, caught in the fractals

of longing. Heat pricks the hair
on the back of his neck;
his whole body's a swarm of bees. That never changes.

All one summer I went down to that song
in the dusty, eucalyptus-pungent
California mountains. . . .

*

Now fireflies, one or two, among the grasses,
in shadows beneath leaves—
like the glint of flesh through a rip

in Glenn Rodgers's corduroy trousers
when at twelve I followed him up the street
past the Berkeley Public Library.

I thought that shy Glenn Rodgers was a god,
his baggy waist-cinched corduroys
and mother-love checked shirt

all the disguise he wore; that inch-long rip
unknown to him,
flapping as he walked, the white flesh gleaming.

*

The light is thick as dust. Around me desk,
bed, books, jumble of stamps, pens, papers.
Good wife, afraid to say I still desire,

still daydream of a man
and luminous shifting hours
where trees came down to the river

thick and twined with multiflora roses,
thickets spangled white,
sweet with a sexual underbite, faintly

acrid like bracken, rain. . . . Afraid
of that old miracle. . . . Desire casts its aura around the body
like the ghostly spiderweb

98

that furred the fallen basswood on the river,
luminous fur on rotting wood. It cracks and snarls
sometimes, like the powerlines we drifted under,

shimmering, lethal— Still, it opens out in me,
floats and shines in the middle distance;
I run my hands over the rough cobble

of dogwood bark, stroke the soft damp golden fringe
at the mouth of a dogtooth violet,
and it is you, and you.

*

Lie side by side, trout and roses, fireflies
and flesh. Carp and flickers, titmice.
Redtailed hawk and great blue heron. Mayflies,

caddisflies, blueflag irises. A man's smile
across the water and your hand's heat
across my side. We touch . . . part.

The guidebook calls them "pernicious invaders,"
but multiflora roses flourish all along the river,
penetrant, sweet. Like bracken, rain.

# A Story About the Lovers and the Lake Bed

*On the bottom of Chewalla Lake,*
*which has been drained, an iron bedstead. . . .*

Then we lay down on the bed
as the waters began to rise.
All night he turned to me and turned to me.
First the faint salt smell of marsh grass
entered our hands, blossomed like stars
from the tips of our fingers. Then fish
began to slither along the channels
of our bloodstreams. Oh the lake came back to life,
calm, green, muddy; I stroked the small hairs
at the back of his neck. Current swirled around the legs,
water rose, lapped us, with a shift and bob
the bed slipped free, then we were floating,
floating, slow waves licking. Along the pines we drifted
until our bleached bones sighed,
turned over in their sleep.
One white egret lifted from the trees.
One blue heron cried beyond the splotched and speckled leaves.
The bedsprings blackened. We fell between the fingers. . . .

# California

This was on Interstate Ten in Los Angeles
and it became, magically, a slow two-lane road
with puddles of water. Stark white leaves,
white trees, leaves floating off the trees,
gravel white beneath, gritty and crunchy
with white leaves; I stopped the convertible
and lay down on the ground, my cheek
next to the water, weeping. And sunlight,
sunlight. Five birds one by one flew in,
settled on a single white branch in a row.
The branch slanted downward toward the water.
One by one the birds, sliding down, lifted off,
wings flashing, and rose into paradise.
I lay down, my cheek against the water,
choking, sobbing, it was too beautiful
for the mind to bear. Suddenly the freeway
with its rushing cars just stopped
and here we were in this backwater road,
the sky blazing clear soft blue, the buildings
morphing back into light, water puddling the road
reflecting light, the grit and pebbliness
of white quartz gravel. White trees lining the road,
shimmery feathery lifting leaves, and white birds
only slightly darker coming in to settle.
Ah, one by one lifting, swoosh, then one,
then one, rapture of gliding then lifting
from the very tips of branches, cars passing
slowly on this two-lane country road. I said to my son,
"I bet you can't believe I'm from here, can you?"

# For Anyone, for You

You roll your burdensome days to the top of the mountain,
then walk home through the crowded city streets
full of the ache you know,
the small lines around your eyes
guarding against your humiliation.

Come to my table and drink my wine.
Then I will cook for you, veal *paprikash* on thick blue plates,
and aromatic rice, and slivers of blood oranges.
We will talk as we wait for night, watching
the shadows grow, the sun as it burns vermilion.

It is so little that I offer, is it all that I can give you?
Did I, becoming sage, give up the power that I once had—
One year the fire ran down my arms from the awakened
chakras, and my hands on the delicate spines
knew what they were doing.

"Your majesty," Cabeza de Vaca wrote, "encounters
have become my meditation." From long crossing on the desert
all his safety burned away and he found
that he could heal, with blind tenderness he
stretched forth his baffled, sunstruck fingers.

When I was young I knew touch was holy.
Delicate, small-boned spines of the bodies of strangers.
I was the lost and found, you could park your grief
and rise up new and radiant in me, as those whom
Cabeza de Vaca touched turned away into the desert, blossoming.

# Notes:

*"Dent de Broc"*
The epigraph, from Villon's "Ballade des Dames du Temps Jadis," translates as "Tell me where, in what country. . . ."

*"Burning"*
"Komm süsser Tod," a phrase from Bach, means "Come sweet Death…"

*"And From the East Like a Long Coffin Being Drawn"*
The title is from a translation by Peter Wirth of Baudelaire's poem "Recueillement."

*"Where, Beneath the Magnolia"*
Rowan Oak is William Faulkner's house in Oxford, Mississippi. Caroline Barr, Faulkner's "mammy," lived to be 100 years old; to her *Go Down, Moses* is dedicated. Teresa Washington, my student and friend, wrote her thesis on the West African religion Ifá.

*"Reiki"*
Reiki is a Japanese healing touch discipline that involves channeling *chi*, the life force, through the laying on of hands. The second section of the poem follows the course of a Reiki treatment.

*"Gala / Milk"*
"Gala," pronounced "yala," is the Greek for milk.

*"For Anyone, for You"*
Alvar Núñez Cabeza de Vaca (1490?-1557?) was treasurer of the Narváez expedition in 1528, which attempted to conquer Florida with 400 men. All but four died in a series of disasters. Cabeza de Vaca wandered through northern Mexico until 1536, traveling from tribe to tribe, and in his solitude discovered his healing powers, which left him once he was reunited with the Spanish. The line is quoted from Haniel Long's "interlinear" translation, *The Power Within*, of Cabeza de Vaca's account of his journey.

# Publication Credits

Many thanks to the editors of the following journals in which these poems appeared, sometimes in different forms:

"The Blessing of My Beloved on My Body," "Blue Window," "Mapplethorpe" —*Feminist Studies*
"California," "Limen," "Dent de Broc," "For Anyone, for You" —*ForPoetry.com*
"Letter from Oxford, Mississippi"—*The Georgia Review*
"Where, Beneath the Magnolia," "What is There to Do in Mississippi?" "Limen"—*Gloria Mundi*
"The Ways He Called Me"—*Iris: A Journal About Women*
"Ice Storm," "And From the East Like a Long Coffin Being Drawn," "Happiness"—*ISLE: Interdisciplinary Studies in Literature and Environment*
"Open Like a Rose"—*The Kenyon Review*
"Between Merced and Morning"—*Natural Bridge*
"Fugue"—*Organization and Environment*
"Light. Olympic Valley, California," "A Story About the Lovers and the Lake Bed"—*Petroglyph*
"The Heirlooms" —*PMS (Poetry, memoir, story)*
"How Death Came To the Horse"—*The Southwest Review*
"*Gala* / Milk," "Stroke"—*The Squaw Review*
"Sweetgum Country"—*The Valparaiso Review*
"What Is There to Do in Mississippi?"—*Wilderness* (Wilderness Society Magazine)
"*Muerto*, 1982," "Wedding *Obi*," "Liège, First Year, First Marriage," "Shorty" —*The Yalobusha Review*

# The Author

Ann Fisher-Wirth lives in Oxford, Mississippi, where she teaches poetry and environmental literature at the University of Mississippi. She is the author of *William Carlos Williams and Autobiography: The Woods of His Own Nature* and of numerous essays on American literature. In 2002-2003 she held the Chair of American Studies at Uppsala University, Sweden. She and her husband Peter Wirth have five children.

## About the Book

This book was typeset in Adobe Garamond, a typeface based on the types of the sixteenth-century printer, publisher, and type designer Claude Garamond (1499-1561), whose sixteenth-century types were modeled on those of Venetian printers from the end of the previous century. The Garamond typeface and its variations have been a standard among book designers and printers for four centuries; nearly every manufacturer of type or typesetting equipment has produced at least one version of Garamond in the past eighty years. Adobe designer Robert Slimbach went to the Plantin-Moretus museum in Antwerp, Belgium, to study the original Garamond typefaces. These served as the basis for the design of the Adobe Garamond romans; the italics are based on types by Robert Granjon, a contemporary of Garamond's.

Book design and composition by JTC Imagineering, Santa Maria, CA.

2882